KITTY CAT LOVE!

KITTY CAT LOVE!

WHY WE LOVE CATS SO MUCH

HOWARD VAN ES

Kitty Cat Love

Why We Love Cats So Much!

Howard VanEs

Published by:

www.booksonhealth.net

ISBN: 978-0615819822

TABLE OF CONTENTS

8 INTRODUCTION

12 HISTORY OF OUR RELATIONSHIP WITH CATS

22 CAT MYTHOLOGY

30 HOW ARE DOMESTIC CATS RELATED TO BIG CATS

36 WHY CATS ARE SO CUTE

40 UNIQUE CAT BEHAVIORS

THE CAT AND HUMAN RELATIONSHIP 48

HEALTH BENEFITS OF CAT COMPANIONSHIP 52

CAT COMEDIANS 56

PLENTY OF PURRSONALITY 62

VARIETY OF CAT BREEDS 64

HAPPILY EVER AFTER 74

ADDITIONAL BOOKS OF INTEREST 80

ABOUT THE AUTHOR 86

INTRODUCTION

"TIME SPENT WITH CATS IS NEVER WASTED"
—SIGMUND FREUD

As any cat lover knows, the comfort and joy found in cat companionship can only be described as transcendental. The bliss of being with, caring and being loved by a cat can perk us up on even the most difficult of days. Cat companionship, quite simply, is one of the greatest joys of life.

According to the 2011-2012 American Pet Products Association's National Pet Owners Survey, Americans own an estimated 86.4 million cats. It's suggested that 33 percent of all American households have at least one pet cat, with 52 percent of those owning more than one.

It will be no surprise to avid cat lovers that these statistics proudly proclaim cats as the number one most beloved pet. And can you really argue with the figures? Not only are cats adorable and highly intelligent, but also have their very own unique, complex and intricate personalities.

And if you're looking for more reasons why we love cats, well simply read on. But first, let's discover exactly how cats clawed their way into our affections.

HISTORY OF OUR RELATIONSHIP WITH CATS :

While the development of the human and cat relationship has definitely been a tumultuous one, it is indisputable that ***today***, some of the greatest animal and human relationships formed are those between cats and people. Sadly this was not always the case. In order to get to where we are now, there were many potholes in the road to cat and human relationship bliss.

According to a study published in *Science* journal, today's housecat descended from *Felis* sylvestris, which is translated as 'cat of the woods'. The authors of the *Science* study estimated that the domestication process, and the beginning of the human and cat relationship, commenced around 12,000 years ago in the Near East.

It is largely believed that a relationship did not form earlier than this simply because humans did not have any use or purpose for cats. Dogs were domesticated far earlier than cats, purely because they were valuable for hunting assistance. But it wasn't until humans settled and begun to store crops and grain that the perception of the value of cats changed.

Once humans started to store grain in large quantities, a problem arose: rats quickly infested the area where grain was stored. Drawn to the potential of huge quantities of live food, cats slunk quietly onto the scene. Without any drama or fuss, the cats hunted the rats and rid the barns of any infestation. Humans were so grateful for the assistance that they left food and treats out for the cats to enjoy as a thank you. And in doing so, humans unconsciously spurred the very first step in the domestication of cats, a process that was unsurprisingly carried out by the cats themselves.

From this point on, cats enjoyed a brief but glorious status as god-like animals. And that is a literal statement – in ancient Egypt cats were so revered that they were often buried with their owners and their lives were even favored over those of a human. In Beni-Hassan, Egypt, archaeologists uncovered a cat cemetery, filled with over 300,000 cat mummies. In fact cats were so revered in ancient Egypt, it's been suggested that , if a human killed a cat, the human was sentenced to death.

During the Middle Ages (and at around the same time of the Black Death) the status of cats was significantly altered. Suddenly, cats became affiliated with witchcraft and evil. Cats, particularly those that were black, were killed en masse.

It's interesting to note that if this treatment hadn't occurred, it's highly likely that the Black Death wouldn't have been as destructive as it was. It's largely believed that rats were the carriers of the bubonic plague and if cats had been allowed to hunt the rats as usual, the plague would never have spread.

However, this is unfortunately not what happened, and the poor treatment of cats continued until around the 1600's when they appeared to regain their usefulness again. With the advent of shipping, cats were brought onboard ships to hunt mice, rats and any other pests that could cause an infestation of the ship.

After this, cats slowly but surely regained their lovable status. Today, cats are considered to be a lucky symbol in Japanese culture. In Burma and Thailand it is an honor to receive a cat as a gift. And worldwide, particularly in the western countries, cats are the most popular pets.

CAT MYTHOLOGY

For as long as cats have had relationships with humans, there have been myths that circulated about these intriguing and independent animals.

One of the most common myths is in relation to the ancient Egyptian goddess, Bast. Bast was the goddess of fertility, protection and the moon. She was also considered to be protector of cats. Depictions of the goddess always portrayed her with the head of a cat, and according to mythology, cats were thought to be the physical manifestation of the goddess Bast.

In Celtic mythology, cats were also highly sacred. Ancient Celts thought that cats were the guardians of the entrance to the Other-world.

Norse legends attributed blessedness to cats and believed that the goddess Frey, who reigned over love, beauty and fertility, used cats to lead her chariot. The Norse took care to feed cats milk in an effort to ensure a good harvest. They also believed that cats were a good luck symbol, and if a cat showed up on the day of somebody's wedding it was thought that the married couple would enjoy a happy life.

HERE ARE A FEW ADDITIONAL MYTHS THAT ARE COMMONLY ASSOCIATED WITH CATS:

- Black cats are allied with witchcraft and Satan.
- Maneki Neko, or the 'beckoning cat' is sacred in Japan and is said to attract good fortune and ward off evil spirits.
- Cats can 'raise the wind' and cause bad weather.
- Cats can drink cows' milk (not true, cats are actually lactose intolerant.)
- A cat can suck the breath from the elderly, ill and young.
- If you put butter on a cats paws it can't get lost.
- Cats always land on their feet.
- Cats have nine lives.

All but one of these myths are false. Can you guess which one? It's actually that the Maneki Neko is a good luck charm – this is true for the Japanese who put their trust and faith in the cat.

As for all of the other myths? False! Yes, even the one where cats always land on their feet. In fact, if a cat is dropped from a low height they may not have enough time to turn and land on their feet. And while their spines are incredibly flexible, dropping them from height may result in death or injury. So if you live in an apartment block, be careful with your furry friend!

HOW ARE DOMESTIC CATS RELATED TO BIG CATS

It's often wondered whether the domestic cats we keep as pets and the big cats we see in zoos are related. After all, they definitely look alike and they share some common traits too. But are they really related?

It turns out that all cats originate from the biological family called Felidae. An individual cat within this family is referred to as a felid. Non-extinct felids come from either the Pantherinae family or the Felinae family.

In the Pantherinae family there are lions, tigers, leopards and jaguars. The Felinae family contains ocelots, cheetahs, cougars, lynxes and

the humble domestic cat. Which means that your furry pet is more closely related to a cougar and a cheetah than they are to a lion and a tiger. That's not to say they're not related at all, as they do originate from the same biological family.

It's interesting to note that during the Ice Age there was another family of cats that existed - the Machairodontinae or saber-toothed cats. This species became extinct approximately 11,000 years. Many sources believe that extinction took place due to the dramatic climate change as well as their species being hunted by humans.

All felids have some common similarities, including the texture and purpose of their tongue and their claws. All cats have slightly prickly tongues that are covered with papillae. This is to assist them in grooming and also in gleaning the meat off their prey. Additionally, all cat species (besides the cheetah), have the ability to protract and retract their claws at will.

So while there are subtle differences in species and breed, it's fair to say that your domestic cat definitely has some shared characteristics with big cats.

WHY CATS ARE SO CUTE

If you were ever unsure of the popularity of cats, all you needed to do was type "cats" into YouTube and sit back as hundreds of cute cat-related videos were fed back to you. Cats truly are the heroes of the digital world, and for good reason too.

So what exactly makes cats so darn irresistible? Is it their tiny noses, their furry ears or even their small size? Well, we'd like to suggest that all of these things make cats adorable and lovable! Here are some other common reasons why cats are so cute.

- The shape and size of their eyes. Much like cartoon characters, their eyes take up a large part of their face and are a central feature of their cuteness.

- Small, delicate paws. Despite being one of their central defense mechanisms, the paws of cats are indescribably cute.

- Their unique, soft coats. It's rare to find two cats with exactly the same markings (besides pure colored cats i.e. black and white) and their uniqueness adds to their cuteness.

- The way they sleep. According to the experts, cats look very similar to toddlers while they're sleeping. This not only adds to their cuteness but also stirs up paternal feelings for the owner of the cat.

- Their signature range of vocalizations. All cats express their emotions differently by using a range of meows. From soft mewing to indignant meowing, the noises cats make are heartbreakingly cute.

UNIQUE CAT BEHAVIORS

Cats interact with humans and the world around them like no other animal. Their behaviors, actions and character traits are uniquely theirs. Which is why we find them so fascinating, and yes, so darn cute.

Read on to discover some cute and unique cat behaviors.

- *Fur ball alert!* While a lot of the hair that cats ingest via cleaning and grooming can be managed by their digestive system, sometimes there is simply too much hair for the cat's body to

deal with or your furry friends tummy is too sensitive to handle the hair overload. When this happens, they will cough up a fur ball to remove the excess hair from the stomach. While the yacking and vomiting isn't too cute, the cuddles and love you get to give them after is definitely worth it.

- *Guardian and protector*. One of the benefits of owning a cat is that they will take care of any unwanted household pests such as mice and cockroaches for you. There are also many accounts of cats alerting their owners to burning houses, burglars and other hazards.

- *Purrs away*. According to research published in the Journal of Zoology (Reference: How cats purr, 2009), the purring

mechanism is actually caused by the laryngeal muscles. Spurred by a neural oscillator, the laryngeal muscles contract to open and close the glottis. Air then hits these vibrating muscles when the cat breathes in and out and results in the purring sound. According to the Journal of Zoology study, purring is not actually a conscious process instigated by the cat. Instead, it's more of unconscious reaction much like a muscular twitch.

Head butt. Called bunting, this behavior is actually a form of communication from your cat. What your cat is effectively doing when she butts against you like this is "scent marking" you as hers.

Bury and cover. We've all seen the way cats bury their poop once they've finished in the litter tray. But why do they do this? One theory is that as instinctive clean freaks, they cover their poop to reduce the "dirtiness" of their environment. Another theory is that poop covering comes from a need to please their owners and to keep their areas clean. It's interesting to note that feral cats do not bury their poop.

Kneading love. It's believed that cats knead (i.e. push rhythmically against something) to express satisfaction and happiness. Mimicking the movements of a kittens getting milk from their mother, this movement is said to symbolize love and a motherly relationship if done on the owner. This brings us to our next chapter: the cat and human relationship.

THE CAT AND HUMAN RELATIONSHIP

More than just a traditional animal and human relationship, the bond between a cat and its owner is both complex and mutually beneficial.

A study published in the journal of Behavioral Processes found that the strong bond between an owner and a cat mimics that of a human relationship, particular when the owner is female. The study also found that cats are as reliant on their owners for food as they are for social interaction.

It also showed that often, the cat can be seen as a furry child in

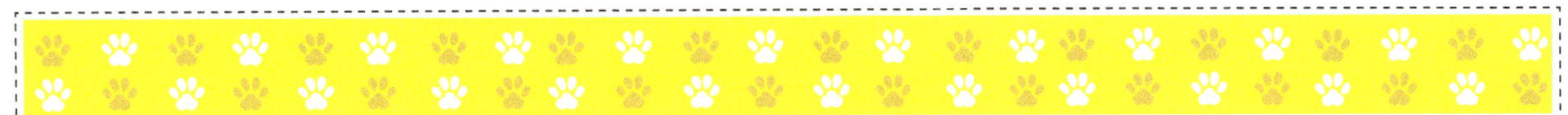

the eyes of the owner, who nurtures and cares for the cat like a parent would. Cats appear to have control over when they are fed by manipulating emotional responses in their owners and using their bargaining power (i.e. food for cuddles or play) to get what they want. Of course, they always remember to return the favor later!

The co-author of the study, Dorothy Gracey from the University of Vienna, stated that the relationship between a cat and human has now been proven to involve affection, play, interaction and social support.

So the next time someone says your beloved pet is just a cat, refer him or her to this study and if you're feeling cheeky, maybe even suggest that your bond with your cat is far deeper than your bond with them!

HEALTH BENEFITS OF CAT COMPANIONSHIP

We all know how enjoyable it is to live with a cat, but did you realize that cat companionship can also positively influence your health and well-being? Here are just some of the health benefits associate with having a cat:

- Decreases stress
- Reduces anxiety
- Boosts your mood
- Helps prevent and treat depression
- Relieves loneliness

- Decreases your risk of cardiovascular disease
- Reduces blood pressure
- Lowers your triglyceride levels
- Decreases your risk of heart attack
- Decreases cholesterol levels
- Prevents against the risk of stroke
- Assists in therapy for autism
- Boosts immune function
- Reduces the risk of developing allergies
- Increases longevity

Source: FutureMedica

CAT COMEDIANS

Despite their regal attitudes, cats can actually be incredibly entertaining and funny. To help highlight their funniness (and give you a bit of a giggle), here are some great cat comedian stories:

- My cat thinks that she has an evil twin that only resides in the bathroom mirror. Every time she sees her own reflection, she puffs up and spits.

- I must have the clumsiest cat in the world. Any time he tries to walk along a thin edge, such as the edge of the sink, he trips over this own feet and only just lands properly! There have been many times when I've seen him trip and land on his butt.

- My cat and I play regular games of hide and seek, taking it in turns to surprise each other. Whenever I find my cat out and find him, he flops on the floor in defeat. Too cute!
- Our cat sees things that we can't see. My partner jokes that she can see dead people, because sometimes she will just jump up and stare at a random spot in the air.
- I know cats are meant to hate water, but I swear my cat can't get enough of it. I have to sneak into the shower and close the door before she can get in, otherwise she hops in and sits at the bottom of the shower with me. She's longhaired, so it takes forever to dry her coat!
- I have both a tabby cat and a golden retriever and they are the best of friends. Our cat follows the golden retriever around and cries when he's not near.

Last Christmas, we bought a giant cat house for our Persian. We spent ages assembling it and putting all the pieces together and when we were finally done, planned on revealing it to our cat. After searching the entire house for him, we found him curled up in the box that the cat house came in, happily sleeping away. To this day, we still have that box and he prefers sleeping in it to the expensive cat house we bought.

Note: all stories have been collected from online forums, personal experiences or testimonials.

PLENTY OF PURRSONALITY

Another reason cats are so loveable is because they each have their own amazing and unique personalities.

While personalities and traits can certainly be breed specific, that's not to say that a specific breed is guaranteed to have a specific personality. Just like different human races have certain personality traits that are typically general, so too do cat breeds. But in the same way that a human can be an individual irrespective of their background or nationality, cats too have unique personalities too. And we love them all the more for it.

VARIETY OF CAT BREEDS

Cat breeds can be separated into three categories: cross breeds, pedigree and non-pedigree. While the number of cat breeds is debatable (different organizations have different opinions on what they accept as a breed) a general figure according to the International Progressive Cat Breeders Alliance is that there are 73 pure breed cat breeds.

While all of the breeds will not be listed here, below are a few of the more popular and family-friendly breeds available.

The most popular breeds according to Animal Planet include:

- ORIENTAL: A domestic cat breed that combines the body type of a Siamese with a wide range of colors and patterns. This talkative cat is curious, intelligent and incredibly playful.
- AMERICAN SHORTHAIR: An undemanding, loving and loyal breed, this cat is just as likely to befriend other animals as it is children. Friendly, non-aggressive and low maintenance.
- BIRMAN: This longhaired and beautiful breed is docile, affectionate and family-friendly. They are a little on the lazy side, but exceedingly relaxed.
- SPHYNX: The sphynx is a high-energy hairless cat that is well known for its affectionate and playful personality. This breed is highly intelligent and curious in nature.

- RAGDOLL: This cross-breed is renowned for its tendency to go limp (like a ragdoll) when carried. With striking blue eyes and soft semi-long hair, this placid and relaxed breed is extremely well loved.

- SIAMESE: Generally considered to be exceedingly extroverted with an abundance of intelligence and curiosity, Siamese are often described as being quite dog-like.

- ABYSSINIAN: Although they aren't considered to be lap cats, Abyssinians are very playful, outgoing and often willful. An exciting and challenging breed.

- EXOTIC: Classified as a short-haired version of the Persian breed, the Exotic is both similar in temperament and look. They are generally calm, curious and friendly with other animals.

- Maine Coon: One of the larger cat breeds, the Maine Coon is also one of the oldest cat breeds too. It's gentle and calm, but also a talented hunter.
- Persian: One of the most beautiful cat breeds, the Persian typically has a long flowing coat and a round face with a shortened nose. It is both calm and relaxed.

And if you're looking for the top ten cat breeds for kids, Animal Planet suggests the following:

1. Persian
2. Abyssinian
3. Maine Coon

4. Siamese
5. Ragdoll
6. British shorthair
7. American shorthair
8. Birman
9. Oriental
10. Sphynx

HAPPILY EVER AFTER

And what do we do once we've found the perfect cat? Well, we spoil them of course. The great thing about living in today's modern world is that there are just *so many* different ways to spoil your beloved pet.

To start with, we pack them off to Kitten Kindy (Kindergarten for cats) where they learn how to socialize with other cats and animals, while getting out and experiencing the big, wide world.

Then we bring them home and dress them up as fairies, princesses and princes. We clad them in tuxedos, denim and bow ties (of course

filming the experience along the way to share with over cat lovers across the globe).

Next, we purchase extravagant, kitty condos, cat trees and cat mansions for our pets to laze around in all day.

Toys, both electronic and fluffy, are bought in abundance and every kind of grooming product available is kept on hand to ensure our pets are always clean and tidy.

There are massage machines to keep our kittens relaxed and stress-free, and specialty made bowls that take care of sensitive whiskers. Cat shelves add interactivity to our modern homes and designer cat beds give them cozy places to sleep.

The abundance of ways to spoil and coddle your cat is truly breath-taking. And as any cat lover knows, ensuring your pet cat is happy and stimulated can never be put in the too hard basket.

Despite their sometimes fussy personalities, sporadic mood swings and begrudgingly given love on the occasional bad day, there are tons of good days when they are caring, playful and heartbreakingly loving. So although they may not have won the “man’s best friend” award (and that is said to be contested over time!), there is no doubt that cats are the most popular and loved pets in world!

ADDITIONAL BOOKS OF INTEREST FROM BOOKS ON HEALTH

DOGGIE LOVE

WHY WE LOVE DOGS SO MUCH!

Explore the divine connection we have with our furry friends through pictures and words. Doggies Love is a celebration of dogs and all the wonderful things they bring into our lives.

AS YOU TURN THROUGH THE PAGES OF THIS DELIGHTFUL BOOK DISCOVER:

- The history of dogs and our early connections
- Why they make us laugh and smile; cuteness factors
- How they reflect the best of our humanity
- Companionship, love, protection, exercise & the many other ways they add to our lives
- And of course, the different ways we spoil them; Like taking them to "Dogya" or the doggie restaurant that serves up Spaghetti Bolognese, made with vegetables and rice!
- Lots of great photos to make your smile, laugh and love our canine companions even more!

If you love cats, you'll love this book!

MEDITATION: THE GIFT INSIDE

HOW TO MEDITATE TO QUIET YOUR MIND, FIND INNER PEACE AND LASTING HAPPINESS

For thousands of years people of faith, ascetics as well as everyday people have practiced meditation to quiet their minds, find inner peace and connect with their spirit.

Whether you are looking for a book on meditation for beginners or you are an experienced meditator wanting to renew your practice you'll find "Meditation: The Gift Inside" connects you to the heart of the practice.

THIS MEDITATION BOOK COVERS:

- How to meditate like a yogi: experience the same meditation techniques that the deepest meditators use.
- Uncover the secrets to quiet your mind; have inner peace even when your outer world may be chaotic.
- Powerful methods to dramatically deepen your meditation.
- How to easily make meditation a part of your daily life and eliminate challenges that may prevent you from practicing regularly.
- Discover how modern scientific research is confirming what the ancient yogis knew about the extraordinary benefits of meditation including: sleeping better, reducing pain, improving mood, extending life, etc.
- Explore the connection between yoga and meditation.
  Order at Amazon.com or www.booksonhealth.net

GERD & ACID REFLUX SOLUTION. YOUR GUIDE TO PREVENTION, TREATMENT, CURES, & RELIEF!

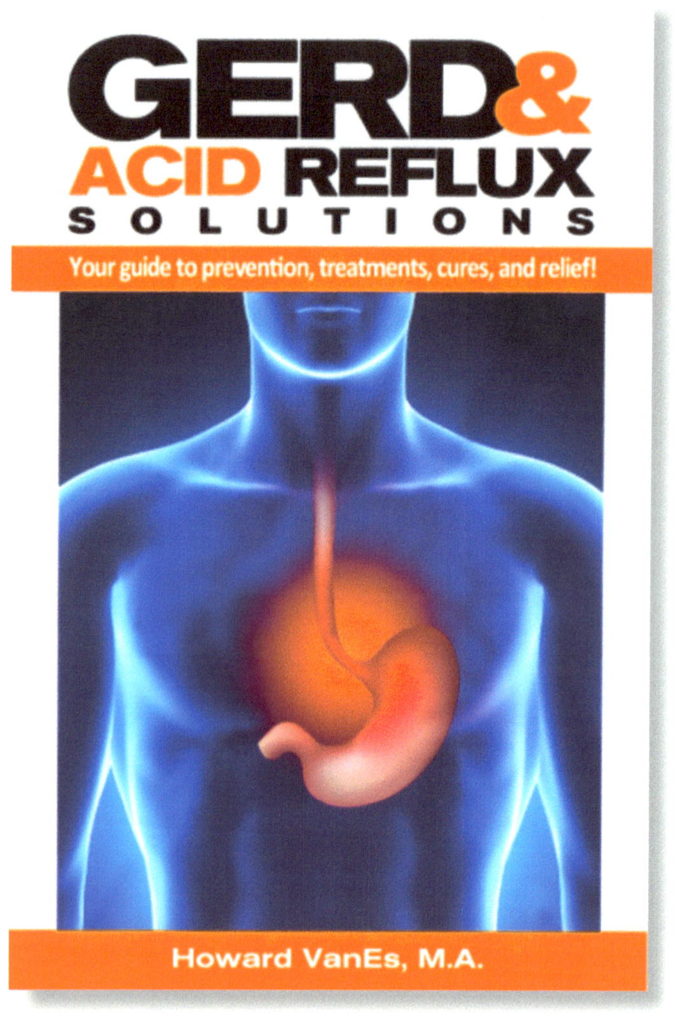

DO YOU SUFFER FROM HEARTBURN OR PERHAPS ONE OF THE OTHER UNCOMFORTABLE SYMPTOMS OF GERD, ALSO KNOWN AS "ACID REFLUX" INCLUDING:

- Unexplained chest pain
- Difficulty swallowing
- Excessive burping & belching
- Frequent nausea & vomiting
- Persistent coughing or hoarseness symptoms
- Laryngitis, sinusitis or ear infections
- Abdominal pain
- Unexplained weight loss
- Dental decay
- Passing of black stool
- Wheezing or asthma-type

And if the physical symptoms of GERD weren't bad enough, you may also lack the joy of eating and socializing, have trouble sleeping, face economic hardship, suffer anxiety associated with medical procedures, and have a reduction in the quality of life.

This book explains why GERD has become so prevalent, provides clear understanding of what is happening inside your body when GERD is present, and gives you with the insight and tools to prevent, reverse and manage it.

IN "GERD & ACID REFLUX SOLUTIONS" YOU WILL DISCOVER:

- How to identify risk factors & warning signs so you can take charge of your health before complications arise.
- Effective prevention strategies.
- How to significantly reduce or eliminate symptoms of GERD with natural alternative treatments such as herbs & supplements as well as easy to make lifestyle adjustments.
- Medical interventions: Prescription and non-prescription medications - how they work and their side effects. And if needed, surgical options are also discussed.
- Which foods aggravate GERD, and which foods are soothing and improve digestion, along with sample recipes that are healthy, delicious and soothing.

ABOUT THE AUTHOR

HOWARD VAN ES is a cat ***and*** dog lover, author of several health and wellness books and yoga teacher living in the Bay Area of San Francisco. Howard is passionate about creating books that inspire, motivate and empower people to live happier and healthier lives.

His deep appreciation for our furry friends and the love and joy they bring into our lives has led him to write ***Kitty Cat Love and Doggie Love.***

Howard can be reached at: Howard@booksonhealth.net

www.ingramcontent.com/pod-product-compliance
Lightning Source LLC
Chambersburg PA
CBHW061353090426
42739CB00002B/13